Hollywood 101™

MAGNIFICENT MONOLOGUES

for kids

by

Chambers Stevens

D0168225

Sandcastle Publishing
South Pasadena, California

Magnificent Monologues for Kids!

Copyright © 1999 by Chambers Stevens
Book Cover & Interior Design by Renee Rolle-Whatley
Book Cover Photography by Karl Preston
The images used herein were obtained from IMSI's Master Clips©/MasterPhotos© Collection, 1895
Francisco Blvd. East, San Rafael, CA 94901-5506, USA

Actors in Photograph: Left-to-Right: <u>Back Row:</u> Peter Esquivel, Lindsey Seibert, Andrew McFarlane, Elizabeth Ishida, Aldis Hodge <u>Front Row:</u> Saroya Whatley, Tyler Seibert, Lauren Schaffel, Travis Tedford

Published by: Sandcastle Publishing & Distribution

Post Office Box 3070
South Pasadena, CA 91031-6070
Phone/FAX (323) 255-3616.

This publication is designed to reflect accurate and authoritative information with regard to the subject covered at the time of publication. It is sold as is, without warranty of any kind, either express or implied, respecting the contents of this book, including but not limited to implied warranties for the book's quality performance, merchantability, or fitness for any particular purpose. The author and publisher assume no responsibility for errors, inaccuracies, omissions or any other inconsistency herein. Neither the author, publisher or its dealers or distributors shall be liable to the purchaser or any other person or entity with respect to any liability, loss, or damage caused or alleged to be cased directly or indirectly by this book. It is sold with the understanding that the book provides educational material and is not rendering other professional recommendations. Any slights against people or organizations are unintentional.

Publisher's Cataloging in Publication
(Provided by Quality Books, Inc.)

Stevens, Chambers.
    Magnificent monologues for kids! / by Chambers
Stevens. -- 1st ed.
      p. cm. -- (Hollywood 101)
      Includes bibliographical references and index.
      Preassigned LCCN: 98-75015
      ISBN: 1-883995-08-6
      SUMMARY: A collection of short monologues for boys
and girls, dealing with such topics as pets, parents,
friends, and school.
      1. Monologues--Juvenile literature   I. Title
PN4305.M6S84 1999   812'.54
                  QBI98-1588

Printed and bound in the United States of America
02 01 00 99   10 9 8 7 6 5 4 3 2

What Others Are Saying About Magnificent Monologues for Kids

"Chambers' monologues are spectacular! Whenever I need a monologue for competition, I go to his book. It's my secret to winning!"
—**ABBY MCFARLANE, 14 YEAR-OLD ACTRESS**
WINNER OF FLORIDA DISTRICT MONOLOGUE COMPETITION

"Chambers' monologues are inventive, whimsical and explosively funny."
—**JIM DELMONT, OMAHA WORLD HERALD**

"Stevens' original monologues range from comedy to drama and everything in between. I strongly recommend *Magnificent Monologues* for aspiring young performers everywhere."
—**MYRNA LIBERMAN, "AUNTIE MYRNA'S KIDS" MANAGEMENT**

"Chambers writes {characters that are} sometimes moving, often funny and always entertaining . . . Chambers Stevens is a superb actor, willing to take risks in pursuit of his goals, stretching *our* imaginations to *his* creative limit as he perfects his craft. "
—**JEFF ELLIS, SOME MAGAZINE**

"I think Chambers knows how to think like a kid. His monologues make sense. I even got a new agent when I did one at an interview."
—**ANDREW HARTER, 8 YEARS OLD**
PRIVILEGE TALENT AGENCY

"Chambers' expertise will take you on a road trip through Hollywood. It's great to have a guide when you go there."
—**BARRY COHEN, EDITOR, NICKELODEON**

"Chambers helped me work on my favorite show, *Rugrats*."
—**BRENNAN LOUIE, ACTOR, 6 YEARS OLD**

"Director Chambers Stevens always draws fine performances from his cast."
—**ANGELA WIBKING-FOX**
NASHVILLE BUSINESS JOURNAL

What Others Are Saying About Chambers Stevens

"Court jester, actor, ring master—kids love him. It is certain he has the gift that draws children to him, and he draws out of them their burgeoning talent."

—SUSAN RUSKIN, EXECUTIVE PRODUCER, *ANACONDA*

"I always see the genuine trust that kids have for Chambers. It allows them to be free in their craft."

—SCOTT DUNCAN, VP, *TRILLION PICTURES*

"Chambers, as a writer/actor, is a man of extraordinary diligence, perception, compassion and talent."

—POLLY WARFIELD, *DRAMA-LOGUE*

"Chambers is a versatile writer/actor of unusual potential. He is a theater professional of high energy and enthusiasm."

—CLARA HIERONYMUS THEATRE CRITIC, *THE TENNESSEAN*

"The Dude [Chambers Stevens] is worth. Way!"

—JAN BRESLAUER, *LOS ANGELES TIMES*

"Children are naturally attracted to Chambers. He has the ability to focus on each child as a person and make them feel that they are special. His success as an acting coach for kids is the result of the knack he has for finding the best in each child and drawing it out with his wonderful sense of fun and enthusiasm."

—TEMPLE LYMBERIS, DIR. OF LEARNING SERVICES, MISSISSIPPI ETV

Table of Contents

Dedication

RUTH SWEET
ACTING TEACHER EXTRAORDINAIRE

"IF YOU ARE NOT HAVING FUN,
THEN WHY ARE YOU DOING IT?"

We are the story tellers. Audiences gather in formal
theatres, in parking lots, in basements, in rooms, in studios,
in places where there are performers sharing stories with
them. The information about our times and society is carried by those who give voice to what writers have scripted.

While that may sound overly dramatic, I suggest that all
we need to do is to look at the pieces contained in these
volumes. Some are serious and some funny. There is non-
sensical writing and whimsical writing. And there is writing
of power and emotion. These are all the sounds of our
times. There is much to laugh about and there is much to
be concerned about. How that information is processed is
the province of the artist. In some form of expression,
artists must voice their feelings about their world. In this
book, in monologue form, there is a kind of representation
of what our present world looks, feels and sounds like.

When viewing monologues in a professional setting as I do,
the first thing I always want to know about is the story— what
is it? And who does it involve? And what is the dramatic
point of the monologue itself as it relates to a story being told
in abbreviated form. Certainly, a monologue is not a whole
play, but it still must have a place to start, an arc to carry the
information forward and an ending that helps to set the sense
of what the story is that we just heard.

Seeing hundreds of pieces like these a year, I am con-
stantly reminded of how clear the story telling must be, how
critical it is that there are some distinct acting and character
choices made and that solid preparation is important to

making the monologue vital and compelling for those watching its presentation. Performing these pieces is just one part of the craft of acting, but making a monologue come alive, may just propel you into being cast.

Auditioning is often a brutal and impersonal part of any performer's life. Being prepared with interesting monologues may bring a sense of security to your work that will serve you well. We are the story tellers and well-told stories get remembered.

Sitting in a tiny New York rehearsal studio casting a play for my theatre with a musical rehearsing on one side and a tap class on the other, I know that our theatrical world is wonderfully absurd and unique. As the Artistic Director of a major regional theatre and a teacher of audition classes, I certainly can see over one-thousand auditions any given year. It isn't necessarily a very glamorous part of the profession. But, when that special combination of spark, joy, connection and risk, gets coupled with emotion and a script, then the excitement of discovering a match of performer to role is a thrilling moment.

Great theatre is about great stories being told and monologues are their own kind of magnificent short stories. For monologues to work there must be clear communication to the audience of the action and intent of the piece. Again, we are the story tellers and well-told stories, such as those in this volume, get remembered.

— STEVEN WOOLF
ARTISTIC DIRECTOR
THE REPERTORY THEATRE OF ST. LOUIS

Welcome to Hollywood 101™, and the wonderful, exciting, magnificent world of monologues.

For the last 12 years, I have been a kids acting coach. Just as Michael Jordan—the world's greatest basketball player—has a coach, many actors do too. I have coached kids in shows for Nickelodeon, Disney, CBS, NBC, ABC, and FOX plus countless movies, commercials and theater productions. I have helped kids get agents, managers, Broadway shows—even the lead in their school play! And in all that time, my biggest challenge has been finding great monologues for young actors.

Did you notice I said, "*great?*" To get the part in a play, movie or even a commercial, "good" isn't good enough. Always strive for magnificent! I call monologues "the olympics of acting." Why? Because when the director says action, it's just you on the stage showing your stuff. For many actors, this is a scary experience. So, when you go on stage, you want to have the best material/script possible, right?! That's what you'll find in this book.

The problem I've found with many other monologue books is, well, the monologues just don't sound like kids talking! They have words and "slang" that I've never heard a kid use. And often they are about very adult subjects that aren't appropriate for kids.

In *Magnificent Monologues for Kids* there are more than 50 monologues all 100% kid tested! They cover a range of subjects, emotions and actions. And best of all, they are fun to perform. Why is that so important? Ask yourself. If acting isn't fun, then why are you doing it?

QUESTION: What is a monologue and why do I need one?

Good question. I'm glad you asked. The short answer is: a monologue is one person talking (unlike a scene, which is two or more people talking).

A monologue is the oldest form of acting. In fact, the first plays written by the Greeks over 2500 years ago, were made up of nothing but monologues. The characters in a play never talked to each other, just to the audience. Can you imagine?

Even Shakespeare used monologues in his plays. His most famous one is in *Romeo and Juliet,* when Juliet, standing on her balcony after the party where she first met Romeo, asks, "Romeo, Romeo, wherefore art thou Romeo?" Almost everyone has heard of that line.

Okay, fine you say. I now know what a monologue is. But why do I need one?

Two reasons really. First, if you are an actor or

actress, which I assume you are, then I'm sure one of your goals is to . . . act! In anything you can: plays, television, film, commercials. Now, the only way you are going to be able to do this is by AUDITIONING. What's that? An actor or actress auditions for directors and producers who make theater, TV and films by showing them how he/she acts. What better way to show them your stuff than to do a Magnificent Monologue. You get it?

Monologues are the easiest dramatic work to audition with. They're short. Audition pieces (another way to describe monologues) should never be longer than two minutes because you don't need another actor, just yourself. I've coached many young actors who won jobs just by performing a great monologue.

The second reason you need great monologues as an actor/actress is also very important. Working on monologues has to be fun! If it's not, it will show in your performance.

In this book, you will meet some of the craziest, silliest, funniest kids I know. Some of them are mean, some of them are sad. And some of the monologues aren't even people talking. But they are all fun to pretend to be.

And if acting isn't fun, then why are you doing it?

Monologues

for

Girls

Susan

(I Love You Aunt Hazel)

(Susan is sitting at her desk. Reading a letter she just wrote.)

Dear Aunt Hazel:

Thank you for the money you sent for my birthday.
It's so nice of you to give me cash every year.
All of my other Aunts give me sweaters and dolls that I
    end up taking back to the store.
But not you.
You are my favorite Aunt.
Every year when the mailman comes and I see your letter,
    I'm always excited.
Except this year.
Why did you only send me a dollar?
What have I done to you except be the perfect niece?
I know times are hard, but a DOLLAR!!!?
What can you buy with that?
Nothing except a candy bar.
And you don't want me to eat candy cause then my teeth
    will rot out and I'll have to get false teeth like you.
A little girl with dentures would look bad.
So please Aunt Hazel, send me more money!

                Your niece,
                Susan

PS. I also take checks.

Lauren
(The Confession)

(Lauren walks up to her mom.)

Mom, I've got something to tell you.
I know sometimes you think I'm a good girl...and I try.
I really try.
But this time...well...I was kind of...well a little bit...bad.
You know when I got mad at you cause you wouldn't let
    me spend the night at Sara's house?
Even though I had done all my chores.
Well I was mad.
Really mad.
Really, really, really mad.
So mad that I did something that I shouldn't have done.
Okay but before I tell you, you've got to promise that
    when you spank me you won't do it too hard.
(Lauren's mom promises.)
Okay.
You know those earrings that dad gave you when you
    first started dating?
The earrings that you always say are the only diamonds
    you own?
Well I flushed them down the garbage disposal.
Someday I hope you can forgive me and you'll think of
    me as you're sweet little girl again.
(She bends over in the spanking position.)
Remember, not too hard.

Stacey
(The Annoying Little Sister)

(Stacey talks to the audience.)

I love being a little sister.
(Makes a really annoying sound. Like a loud car alarm.)
Annoying isn't it.
I do it to my brother all the time.
He gets real mad and tries to hit me.
But I yell, "Mom! Drew is trying to hit me!"
And that makes him stop real quick.
Isn't that great?
I do lots of mean things to my brother.
When his girlfriend calls, I tell her, "Drew's not here. He
    had a big date tonight!"
And then when his friends that are boys call, I say, "Sorry
    he can't come to the phone. He's on a date with your
    girlfriend."
So far I've got my brother beaten up three times.
I love being a little sister!

Amy
(My Sister Ran Away)

(Amy is sitting on her bed holding a necklace.)

Last night my sister ran away.
Her and mom got into a big argument.
They were screamin' and yellin'. Ever since my dad died,
    they fight a lot.
But this was the worst ever.
After awhile my sister went to her room and slammed
    the door.
I thought it was all over, so I went to bed.
But later that night my sister woke me up and told me
    she was running away.
She said she loved me.
But she couldn't live with my mom.
And then she gave me her necklace. The one that dad
    gave her for her birthday.
She said it was so I would never forget her.
And then she left.
Mom is still asleep.
But when she wakes up she is going to be very mad.
I don't know what to do.

Erin
(The Beanie Baby Brat)

(Erin is sitting on the stage surrounded by Beanie Babies.)

My brother calls me a brat.
He says I never do anything nice.

But that is a lie.
I do nice things for my Beanie Babies

Don't you just love Beanie Babies?
I do.
Love'em. Love'em. Love'em.
And not to collect them.
To play with them.

I have about a hundred.
I keep getting my grandma to buy me more and
    more and more.
Last week she said that she wasn't going to buy me
    anything else.
So I pretended to be sick.
And she bought me ten more Beanie Babies.

My favorite is Chip the Calico Cat.
He can beat up my brother's Power Ranger.
Scratch his eyes out.
Boy do I love Beanie Babies.

Okay, maybe I am a brat.

Karen
(The Best Way to Trick Your Parents)

(Karen is giving her best friend Lindsey some advice.)

Listen Lindsey,
You're doing it all wrong.
If you want your parents to do everything you say,
    you have to follow the rules.
Look, stop crying you big baby or I'm not going to
    help you.
All right, that's better.

Okay. Rule number one: whine
Whine!
Whine!
Whine!
Whining is a kid's best friend.
(Whining) "Dad I have to have the Princess Diana Beanie
Baby. What's 400 dollars when your love your daughter?"

Rule number two: lie!
Lie!
Lie!
Lie!
(Really excited) "No Dad, your toupée looks really good
    on you."
"Whoa Mom, have you lost some weight! Like at
    least 50 pounds."

(cont. next page)

Karen
(The Best Way to Trick Your Parents cont.)

"Wow Grandma. Your mustache is totally gone!"

And rule number three: be full of surprises.
Like just when they think you're a little spoiled brat,
    do something nice...really nice.
Like help your mom cut her toenails.
I know it's disgusting.
But being a kid ain't pretty.

Follow these rules and you'll rule the house.
I've got to go. I'm helping my grandma shave her back.

Mae
(Coaching the Team)

(Mae is the captain of the softball team. She is yelling at the team.)

Listen up girls!
Lauren. Stop doing your nails and listen to me.
The score is tied 4 to 4.
No thanks to you Amanda. You strike out one more
    time and I'm going to tell Ryan you have a crush on him.
What?
You do.
Everybody knows it.
Right girls.?
(The girls yell)
See. Okay, so it's 4 to 4.
We can win. I know we can do it.
Lauren. Stop doing your nails!
What it is with you people?
We're trying to play a game here.
Brittney! Stop staring at the boys.
You people are hopeless.
Now listen up.
It will be the first time in my life that the girls have beat
    the boys in softball.
Thanks to Jennifer's homerun, we're tied.
So ladies, if you'll just keep your eyes on the ball and not
    on the young boys, I know we can cream them . . .

Not you Lauren. Your nails are wet. You'll have to sit
    out this inning.
So go out there ladies and score, score score!

Maggie
(A Dream)

(Maggie is talking to the audience.)

I had the weirdest dream last night.

I was like Snow White and I had these 7 little people around me.

But they didn't carry picks and shovels like the dwarfs in the movie.

Instead, they carried guitars and drums.

It seemed we were like a rock band.

And I was the singer, which is strange cause I didn't even know I could sing.

And we were performing in front of this castle for the king...who looked a lot like Scooby Doo.

And we sang, "Row, row, row your boat."

We sang it really fast.

And every one danced around.

And I danced with Scooby Doo!

And we danced so fast that we didn't see where we were going.

And we danced over the bridge and fell in the moat!

And that's when I woke up and noticed my dog, Sloppy, was licking my face.

Morgana
(We were Robbed)

(Morgana is talking to the audience.)

Last night my parents took my little sister and me
    to the movies.
It was THE PARENT TRAP.
And on the way home, my sister and I were laughing a
    lot, wondering what it would be like to be a twin.
When we got to our house, we noticed the front door
    was open.
Somebody had robbed us.
Inside, it looked like a tornado went right through our
    living room.
They took our television, computer and all my
    mom's jewelry.
My dad called the police and they came really fast.
They said they will try to get our stuff back.
When they left my mom said it was time for us to
    go to bed.
My sister said she was too scared to sleep.
So I had to sleep in the bed with her.
I was glad cause I was scared too.

Robin

(Problems with a Copycat)

(Robin is talking to the audience.)

My best friend, Lisa, is the biggest copycat in the world.
Everything I do, she copies.
And I'm sick of it.
Last week, I got a great Levi's jacket.
And today in school, what does Lisa have on?
A Levi's jacket.
I asked her if she was trying to copy me and she said,
    "No way. I've had this a long time before you."
Can you believe she lied like that?
So I was like "Whatever".
And then she got really mad and said that "Whatever"
    was her word,
And that I was copying her by saying it.
Like that is totally not true.
I started using "Whatever" when I saw CLUELESS.
And I remember that I saw it two days before she did.
So I tell her that and she says, "Forget it" and storms off.
"Forget it?"
That's what I always say when I get mad.
She is such a copycat.
Why am I telling you this?
Just forget it.
(Robin storms off)

Pearl
(Grandmas are Cool)

(Pearl is talking to the audience.)

My favorite person in the whole world is my grandma.
She is so cool.
Every time I go to her house, we do something fun.
We bake cookies.
And not boring ol' chocolate chip cookies.
No, we bake peanut butter, oatmeal raisin cookies
    with M & M's.
Next time I see you, I'll bring you some.
Oh, and sometimes we dress up in all her old clothes.
She has the wildest hats.
And we have a tea party.
And she invites all her old friends and they come over
    in their wild hats and we have a blast.
But the best thing about grandma is when we just sit
    and talk.
Sometimes I tell her when mom and dad make me mad.
And you know what she says?
She says, "Honey, I totally understand. Sometimes your
    mom and dad make me mad too!"
My grandma is so cool.

Breanna

(The Nightmare)

(Breanna is reading her book report before the class.)

My book report is on "The Beast" by R. L. Stine.
R. L. Stine is a writer of the Goosebumps books.
I've never read a Goosebumps book before so I decided
to do my book report on this one.

The book is about...well it's about...Wait! *(Throws down her paper.)* I'm sorry. I can't do this. Mrs. Higgins, I didn't read "The Beast." I started it last night before I went to sleep but the first chapter was so scary. I couldn't turn the next page. I sat there frozen in fear like this: *(She opens her mouth in a look of terror.)* All night I was scared that Frankenstein, Dracula, The Wolfman, or some mummy was going to break into my room and get me. When the sun came up I ran to my parents' room and jumped into their bed. So Mrs. Higgins, I know you have to give me a bad grade. But can I make it up by reading something silly like Pippi Longstocking?

Heidi

(Present from Korea)

(Heidi is talking to the audience.)

Today I got a new baby sister. She doesn't look anything like me. She's got black hair and dark eyes and she doesn't even look like my mom or dad. We didn't get her from the hospital, we got her from the airport. Last night we got a call from the adoption agency that my new sister will be arriving from Korea early this morning! I was scared. I've been an only child for a long time. I didn't know if I wanted a new sister. So we're standing at the airport with all these other families that are waiting for their babies. And we waited for hours. Finally, the airplane door opened and all these nurses came out holding little bundles. And each one had a name pinned on its blanket. After what seemed like forever, a nurse came out holding my sister. She handed her to my mom and dad and they started to cry. I didn't want to look. But then my mom handed her to me and I saw the most beautiful face I've ever seen. Wow. Today I became a big sister.

Kathryn

(The Ultimate Shopping Mall)

(Kathryn talks to the audience.)

When I grow up, I'm going to be the richest person in the world! I'm going to have millions and millions and millions of dollars. I'll have so much money that I'll have to hire a whole football team just to carry my wallet. The first thing that I'm going to buy is a gigantic house. It'll have two stories. I'll live upstairs. And downstairs will be a mall. I'll call it "Kathryn's Gigantic Fun Mall." So whenever I need new clothes, I just go down there and pick them out. Next door to my house, I'll have my own **Toys 'Я' Us.** But instead of boys' and girls' toys, it'll just have girl toys. And I'll invite my friends over to play. And when they leave, I'll give each one a brand new Barbie!

Oh! And I'll have my own private cook, too! And all he'll make is pizza. Cheese pizza 'cause that's my favorite. Oh and I'll own an ice cream store, too. But instead of 31 flavors I'll have 131 flavors. And I'll have lots of parties and invite my friends. And I'll even invite people who used to be mean to me to show them I'm not stuck up. I can't wait to be rich. Oh, that reminds me, can I borrow a quarter? I need to make a phone call.

Saroya
(Where Oh Where is My Cat?)

(Saroya is looking for her cat.)

It's not my fault.
Well, it is my fault.
But I didn't mean it.
My cat, Winston.
He ran away.
And my mom is blaming me!
She said I should have fed him when I was supposed to.
I was gonna.
But . . . Rugrats was on TV.
And it was a good one, too.
See Angelica, she tricked the babies into playing this
    detective game and...
Well, it wasn't that good actually.
Not as good as my cat.
(Calling) Winston!
Where is he?
I'm worried about him.
Maybe he went outside and some mean old robbers
    stole him.
And maybe they will take him to Hollywood.
And maybe someone will see him and put him on a
    commercial and then I'll turn on the TV.
And there he'll be and he'll be rich and happy and never
want to live with me again.

(cont. next page)

Saroya
(Where Oh Where is My Cat? cont.)

I didn't even feed him.
(Calling) Winston!
Oh.
I wish I had fed him like I was supposed to.
I'm such a bad girl.
(She sees Winston walking toward her.)
Winston?
(Giving him a hug.)
Oh. Winston!

Leslie
(Being Beautiful is Hard)

(Leslie is talking to a friend.)

People think models are stupid!

Yeah, right.
If we're so stupid, how come we're so rich?
How do you think we got all that money . . . our looks.

Hey, it's not easy being this beautiful.
I have to sleep a lot so I don't get bags under my eyes.
Sleeping is very hard work.
I have all these dreams . . . it's a nightmare.

And people think models are dumb, too.
I'll have you know I am graduating from 8th grade
    with a C average.

The biggest problem with being a model is the guys.
They are always hitting on us.
But I tell them I don't date non-models.
See, I need a boyfriend who is as least as good-looking
    as me.
You understand, right?

(cont. next page)

Leslie
(Being Beautiful is Hard cont.)

(Small laugh) Well no, of course you don't understand.
You're kind of homely looking. But that's cool.
In a way, homely is kind of better.

Like see, I'm beautiful.
And if I work really really really hard I'll be really
    really really beautiful.
But you, no matter what *you* do, are still homely.
So, you get to skip all the hard work.
Gosh, I envy you.

Lindsey
(I'm a Star)

(Lindsey is a young bratty actress talking to her mom.)

Commercials! Commercials! Commercials!
I am sick and tired of commercials!

I have sold everything under the sun: detergent, diapers, toys, food, more diapers, cars, soft drinks, and even more diapers. In Hollywood, people call me "The Diaper Queen." I've done spots for whip cream, French toast, hamburger, hot dogs and tacos even dogs wouldn't eat. And believe it or not, I've even done a job for toilet paper. That was a low point in my career. So look, if you send me on another commercial audition, I'll scream.

I want to be a movie star. The biggest movie star the world has ever seen. I'll be right up there with Leonardo DeCaprio. When he meets me, he is going to have a terrible crush on me.

No Leonardo. I can't hold your hand. I'm only ten.

Oh and I want to be in musicals too. I'll sing and dance: ballet, jazz, modern. I'll even tap dance on pianos. And everyone in the theatre will stand up and cheer.

(cont. next page)

Lindsey
(I'm a Star cont.)

(Talking to the audience.)

"No please, sit down. It's now time to sing my ballad."
That's the slow song. Oh and I'll do concerts, too.
Sell out Carnegie Hall for a month. Barbara Streisand
will be so jealous. Watch out world, here comes the
biggest star you have ever seen.

So Mom, you better be nice to me.
'Cause when I'm famous, I'll be the boss.

Gertie
(Cats are Cool)

(Gertie is a cat.)

Meow. Meow.

Being a cat is sooo cool. 'Cause cats can do whatever they want whenever they want. If I want to sleep all day, then I do. Not like a dog who always has to run and play. If I don't feel like doing anything, I don't. 'Cause I'm a cat. No one expects me to catch a stick. And if my owner gets mad at me because I've been clawing the furniture or coughed up a hairball in his bathtub, I just climb a tree and hide. Being a cat is cool.

Meow. Meow.

Betsy
(I'm Adopted)

(Betsy is talking to the audience.)

My mom and dad won't admit it, but I think I'm adopted. It's obvious, too. I mean, look at all the differences. I'm beautiful and my parents look . . . weird. I'm smart and my parents aren't . . . smart. Let's just say the lights are on but nobody's home. I don't want to rag on them or anything. They've done a pretty good job raising me. But I think it's time for me to find my real parents. My birth parents. I'm sure they're rich. My dad is handsome and my mom is a supermodel. And they'll come pick me up in their jet and we'll fly to Paris, where they'll get me new clothes for school. Then we'll fly to their mansion and I'll have my own room with an indoor swimming pool where me and my sister can swim.

Wait a minute! What about my sister? If I go, then I'll have to leave my sister. And wait a minute . . . I don't want to change schools. I just made the cheerleading squad. Hey! They better not come here thinking they can buy me off! They're the ones that gave me up all those years ago. I mean hey, my mom and dad may not be my birth parents, but at least they stuck by me when I got sick. Who do these people think they are? I guess I better not look for them. It'll just cause too many problems.

Leanna
(The Science Project)

(Leanna runs into her parents bedroom and turns on the light.)

Dad! Dad wake up! I need your help! *(Leanna's mom starts to wake up.)* Go back to sleep, Mom, I just need Dad. *(Dad is still not up.)* Dad please wake up and come downstairs and help me! My science project is due tomorrow and I haven't even started! I can't believe I forgot. I was asleep and I was having this dream about flying to Los Angeles to swim in the ocean. It was a great plane and the stewardess was talking about how cold the ocean was in November. And then I remembered. Ocean?! I've got a science project due on the 15th. And today is the fourteenth. No, it's 3 am! So TODAY is the 15th. And my big science project, the one that is half of my science grade, is due in 5 hours! *(Leanna's dad is still lying there)* Dad get up! You were always good in science. I know you can think of something! I told the teacher I was going to raise two goldfish. One goldfish I was going to feed fish food from the store. And the other one I was going to feed live worms. I told her I would do this for a couple of months. And then on November 15th, when the project was due, I would see which fish was bigger. Thus proving that . . . well I don't know what it will prove. It just better prove something! But Dad I forgot to get the goldfish from the store. So I need you to get up, get dressed,

(cont. next page)

Leanna
(The Science Project cont.)

get your fishing gear and take me to the lake so we can catch two fish. I'll just tell my teacher they were once goldfish but the gold fell off. I can't believe I forgot my project was due November 15th. I felt I had more time. Get up!

(Her dad mumbles something.)

What? It's October! Where did I get the idea this was November? *(Laughing)* Oh yeah. The stewardess in my dream said it was November. Well I better go back to sleep and tell her she has the wrong month. Sorry Dad. I hope I didn't wake you up. *(Leanna's dad is still not moving.)* Dad? Oh well. Sweet dreams.

Stephanie
(The Kickball Queen of the World)

(Stephanie comes running on stage shouting.)

I am the kickball queen of the world! You guys should've seen me. I kicked four homeruns in a single game. *(Chanting)* I am queen! I am queen! Do you know how to play kickball? It's like baseball only instead of using a bat you use your feet. It's harder than it looks. See, today at the playground, a bunch of high school kids came over and laughed at us for playing kickball. They said it was a sissy game. So I said "Yeah? Well this sissy *(pointing to herself)* can beat you anytime, any day." And they were like "Yeah. Right." So they played us in a game. They didn't have a chance. I got all the middle school kids and we beat them 22 to 7! And that's counting my four homeruns. I am the kickball queen of the world! I wonder if they have kickball in the Olympics?

Princess Polly

(You Got to Kiss a Lot of Frogs to Make a Prince)

(She enters kissing a frog.)

Come on! Come on! Turn into a prince. (Kissing it again) What's wrong with you? Now look, I'm a princess and I've got better things to do than sit here all day kissing a toad. Come on! I was in the woods and I saw that old ugly witch . . . what's her name? You know, the one with the warts. Anyway she turned you from a handsome prince into this toad. And everyone knows the only way you can turn back into a boy is for a beautiful princess to kiss you. And if I know one thing, I'm beautiful. *(Kisses him again.)* Oh, come on! The big ball is in a couple of hours and I need a date.

That's the worst thing about being a princess. All the guys are scared to ask me out. They're scared that if they do something stupid on the date, I'll have their heads cut off. Ok, I only did that one time. I don't understand why you're not changing into a prince. Let me look into my princess handbook to see if I'm doing this right. *(Turning pages of book.)* Let's see—"How To Weave Straw Into Gold"—"How To Catch A Man With One Glass Slipper"—here it is—"How To Change A Frog Into A Prince." *(Reading)* Kiss it! That's what I'm doing. Wait, there's more. Warning: Make sure the frog is NOT a toad. Toads never turn into a prince. They just cause warts and make you look like witches. Uh oh, I'm in trouble!

Mary-Joe
(The Clothes Make The Girl)

(Mary-Joe enters in a T-shirt and jeans.)

Mom, how do I look? Now be honest because the first day of school is important. I want to look happy, fun, the life of the party. But not silly or stupid. Enough people think of me that way already. I want to look beautiful, pretty, gorgeous but I don't want to look like I'm trying to be beautiful, pretty, or gorgeous. I want boys to look at me and say "Hey! I want to ask her out." But I don't want them to get the wrong idea. How come boys always get the wrong idea? I want to look smart but not too smart. I mean, I don't want to look like a genius or anything. So Mom, do you think that this outfit says that I am friendly, smart, pretty, available? Or does it make me look grouchy, unattractive, dumb, and desperate? I gotta know Mom. And hurry, the bus will be here in 5 minutes!

Allie

(It's That Time Again)

(Allie rings doorbell.)

Hi, Mrs. Seibert. Guess what? It's that time of year again. Our school is selling magazines! Now, let's see. Last year you got *Readers Digest, Ladies Home Journal, Time,* and *Rolling Stone.* So I'm sure you'll want to get all those again. We're having a special on *People.* Only a dollar a week! *(Mumbles)* If you buy *TV Guide* at regular price— What? Now Mrs. Seibert, don't start with that. We go through this every year. The magazines help the school buy books, supplies, and sends us to Disney World for a week every year. Oh, don't give me that. You're not broke! I've already called the bank. You have at least $7,000. in your checking. Not counting your savings. But hey, look, don't let me pressure you. If you don't want to buy any magazines, fine. But don't blame me if rumors start going around town that you and Mr. Seibert hit the booze a little too often. I would hate for the preacher to find out what kind of person you really are. Oh Mrs. Seibert, stop crying . . . it's okay. I'll just put you down for all the magazines you had last year plus the *People* and the *TV Guide.* Now you feel better? Okay well, I gotta go. See you next week. I'm helping the band sell candy.

Cindy

(My Mom is Sick)

(Cindy is talking to the audience.)

My mom is in the hospital. She's been in there over a month. My dad and I have gone to see her everyday, and even though we don't say it, I think she's looking worse. I thought hospitals were supposed to make you better. Mom says not to worry about her. She says she's strong and she can beat the cancer. I hope she's right. At night sometimes I wonder what'll happen if she dies. What'll I do? What will my dad do? I try not to think about it because it'll make me cry. And I'm scared if I start crying I may never stop.

Scarlett
(There's No Such Thing As Monsters)

(Scarlett is sitting on the edge of her bed.)

Every night my little sister goes through the same thing.
First, our parents tell her and me to go to bed. I always
put my pajamas right on. But my little sister cries and
cries. She hates going to bed. She says there are monsters in her room. Yeah right. Then dad has to carry her
to her room. And look in the closet and under the bed
and show her that there are no monsters hiding. And
then finally she goes to sleep. Isn't that stupid? What
kind of monsters could fit under a bed? Does she really
think there are big green slimy creatures hiding in her
room. That's stupid. *(She looks around the room.)* Dad!
Can you come in here. I think something's under my
bed. Hurry!

Monologues

for

Boys

Chuck

(I Can't Read)

(Chuck walks up to his teacher.)

Mr. Barry?

I need to talk to you.

It's about my grades.

I've been trying real hard to do my homework.

If I bring home a bad report card, my dad will kill me.

Well, not kill me, but he'll be mad.

And Mr. Barry, when my dad gets mad, everybody in
my family runs.

Even my mother.

So I want to get good grades . . . but I'm having a real
hard time.

Mr. Barry, I can't read.

I never learned how.

In most classes it doesn't matter 'cause I cheat.

But in your class, you watch us all the time . . . and that's
why I'm making bad grades.

Mr. Barry, I don't want to cheat anymore.

I want to do good.

Can you teach me to read?

Jeremy
(Where are the Kids?)

(Jeremy walks up to door and knocks. The door opens.)

Uh . . . Hi. My name is Jeremy and I just moved into the
neighborhood today and I was wondering if you have
any kids?

See, I've been riding my bike up and down the street for
the last couple of hours and I haven't seen a single kid.

And I'm starting to get worried.

Back in Florida where I'm from, there were tons of kids.

And we always played outside.

You know, roller skating, throwing baseballs, playing tag.

But here . . . well . . . it's quiet.

Too quiet.

I haven't even seen a stray dog.

So lady you understand I'm starting to get nervous.

This is not a town with just old people in it, is it?

(He hears a noise of a bus pulling up.)

Hey, what's that?

A school bus?

All the kids were at school?

In the summer?

Boy, this is a crazy town.

Andrew
(Wiggling for Grandpa)

(Andrew is talking to the audience.)

I don't have a grandpa.
I used to have one before I was born.
But he died.
Grandma said, "He was a great guy".
He liked to fish.
I have a picture of him holding up a shark almost as
    big as me.
And he could wiggle his ears.
Sometimes Grandma misses him.
And she starts to cry.
I'm trying to learn to wiggle *my* ears.
Maybe that will make her feel better.
(He tries to wiggle his ears.)
Is it working?

Avery
(The Baseball Game)

(Avery's pretending he's pitching the big game. He has a wild imagination.)

Here he is, the greatest pitcher in the world!
Avery!
The crowd goes wild as he steps up to the mound.
He leans back and lets that ball rip.
Strike one!
Boy he is pitching great today.
Strike two!
Wow, that ball was so fast I didn't even see it go across
    the plate.
Strike three!
The batter's out-of-there!
The crowd goes wild. Avery has done it again.
Pitched his one millionth no-hitter!
Wait, look!
The fans are coming on to the field.
I can't believe this!
They are picking Avery up and carrying him around
    on their shoulders.
Boy do they love their pitcher!
(Avery looks at the audience.)
What?
It could happen like that.
Today is my first day to pitch a real game.
The coach says I'm ready.
My dad says I'm ready.
How come I don't feel ready?

Derrick

(I Need a Nintendo 64)

(Derrick is talking to the audience.)

Have you ever wanted something so bad that if you didn't
   get it you would die?
Me, too!
I want a Nintendo 64.
But my mom just doesn't understand.
I tell her if I don't get a Nintendo 64, my head is going to
   swell up, turn green and explode.
You'd think that would convince her.
But nooooooooooooooooo!
She says video games are too violent and they'll
   make me crazy.
(Throwing a big tantrum)
No they won't!
No they won't!
No they won't!
I've tried everything to convince her.
I've even worked around the house to earn money.
Me, work!
Can you imagine?
Horrible.
I wouldn't recommend it.
But after a day's work, all she gave me was a quarter.
A quarter?
(Yells offstage to his mom.) This is not 1938!
Look, you are my only hope.
Give me a Nintendo or I'll explode.

Nick

(I Need a Dad)

(Nick is talking to the audience.)

Work, work, work.
All my dad does is work.
He wastes every weekend working on a house
    he's trying to sell.
He's always painting or mowing or going to the hardware
    store.
I never see him without a hammer in his hand.
He's missed my last 6 soccer games!
Even the 2 goals I made in the district finals!
He says he's sorry.
And next time, he'll come to the game.
But he never does.
All for a stupid house.
My mom is even getting tired of it.
She's always naggin' him to spend more time with me.
But dad says we need the money, so he has to work hard.
Well maybe . . . but I need a dad more.

Steve

(The Big Excuse)

(Steve walks into the classroom . . . late!)

Hey Teach.

Sorry I'm late but the strangest thing happened to me
    on the way to class.

I was just walking along on the way to the school bus
    when . . . uh . . . a circus came by.

It was like a circus parade.

And the next thing I knew, one of the elephants wrapped
    his trunk around me and put me on his back.

Well, I started screaming 'cause I wanted to get to
    school.

But no one could hear me 'cause the marching band was
    playing so loud.

I tried to jump down but . . . have you ever tried to get
    down from a moving elephant?

It's not easy.

After about an hour, the elephant stopped and a clown
    on stilts walked by and helped me down.

And I ran all the way to class.

So sorry I'm late but I guess you understand that when
    an elephant grabs you, you have to do what it wants.

Rob

(Beating Up the Bully)

(Rob comes running up to his grandpa.)

Grandpa?
Grandpa?
Where are you?
There you are.
I did it!
I did it!
Just like you said.
Oh Grandpa is was great!
You would have been so proud of me.
See, it was after school and Billy Thomas was behind the
    bleachers beating up kids like usual.
He was picking on this one 5th grader who is so much
    smaller than him.
So there is this crowd around the fight and I walk up and
    say, "HEY!"
Everybody turns around 'cause they think it is a teacher.
But when Billy sees me he says, "Hey Squirt, you better
    get out of here cause I'm going to beat you up next."
And everybody laughs 'cause Billy has beat me up a lot.
But before they can start fighting again I say, "So?"
Just like that.
And Billy looks over and says, "Hey Runt, I said get out
    of here."

(cont. next page)

Rob

(Beating Up the Bully cont.)

And I just say, "So?"
Billy then pushes me and I'm on the ground and he stands
    over me and goes, "You are in big trouble now".
I look him right in the eyes and go, "So."
Billy starts freaking out. He's yelling, "Why do you keep
    saying that. Your mother is stupid."
Everyone thought this would really make me mad.
But I just say, "So."
And then everyone laughs 'cause that made Billy
    really mad.
And then he started calling me lots of names and all
    I said was, "So. So. So".
Grandpa, you should have seen him.
He was mad!
So mad that he started to cry and he ran away.
And everybody cheered.
And the little 5th grade kid was really happy.
You were so right Grandpa.
Bullies need people to be scared of them.
And when you're not, well, they turn into the big babies
    they are.

Ty

(Watch Out for that Car!)

(Ty is talking to the audience.)

Yesterday my dog, Freckles, got hit by a car.
Me and Freckles were outside playing Stickbite.
Do you and your dog play that?
We play it all the time.
I throw the stick and he gets it and brings it back.
But then, before he gives it to me, Freckles runs around
    and makes me catch him.
And when I do, I have to pull the stick out of his mouth.
He has a very strong mouth.
That's why we call it Stickbite.
Well yesterday, I threw the stick and Freckles caught it
    in mid-air.
He's never done that before.
And I guess he was so excited, he didn't notice that he
    ran out into the street.
And then he got hit by a car.
It was the scariest moment of my life.
Oh don't worry, he didn't die.
He just had to go to the hospital and get a cast
    for his broken leg.
He's inside lying down resting.
I guess it will be awhile before we can play Stickbite again.

Warner
(Grounded Again)

(Warner comes stomping into the room slamming the door on the way. Then he goes back to the door, opens it—)

(Yelling) GROUND ME, I DON'T CARE!
(He slams the door again and looks at the audience.)
I'm grounded again.
It's the third time this week.
And it's not even my fault.
(He goes back and opens the door.)
IT'S NOT MY FAULT!
My Mom blames me for everything my sister does.
Breanna is always getting me into trouble!
A couple of days ago, she took my mom's best lamp and
threw it down the stairs.
What a mess.
And then yesterday, she put a metal fork into the
    microwave and nearly caught the kitchen on fire.
Then today, she put her finger-paints into the washing
    machine.
Now all my dad's shirts are pink.
And my Mom blamed everything on me.
I try to tell her it's not my fault.
But Mom says I told Breanna to do all those things.
And that is not true!
What I DID tell Breanna is it would be cool if she did all
    those things.
Which is NOT the same thing!
It's not my fault she wants to be cool.

Tanner

(No Meat for Me)

(Tanner is talking to the audience.)

Hi. My name is Tanner and I'm a vegetarian. A lot of kids my age don't even know what a vegetarian is. When I tell kids they usually say, "Oh, your parents are vegetarians, too?" Nope, just me. Everyone else in my family eats meat. Then people say, "Why are you a vegetarian?" Um, well it all started last May when my class went on a field trip to a dairy farm. Everybody in my class got a cow to milk and at first it was really cool. My cow was named Bessie. You should have seen how much milk she made. And she let me pet her and I even got to hear her moo. It was great! *(Imitating a cow)* Moo! On the way home from the field trip we stopped for lunch at a hamburger place. Just as I was about to bite in a big juicy cheeseburger, I thought, "Wait a minute . . . this could be Bessie." So that's when I started to be a vegetarian. Next week I'm going back to the farm to visit Bessie.

Rusty

(The Life of a Dog)

(Rusty runs on stage and yells, then runs back off stage.)

Where is it? I don't see it. I can't find the stick! I hate being a dog. Run, get this. Run, catch this ball! Good job boy, good job. Here's a bone. A bone? Where did humans ever get the idea that dogs like bones? How about some meat? What I wouldn't give for a good hamburger right now. *(Scratching)* Got this flea that's been bothering me for a whole week. *(Scratching even harder.)* I'll get ya! There, he's gone! I hate those little boogers. *(Yells off stage.)* What? No, I'm still looking. *(Looking at audience.)* If he wants his stick so bad why won't he come look for it himself? Agh, people! They may think we're their best friend, but my best friend is a hamburger.

Prince Patrick
(Slaying the Dragon)

(Prince runs on stage.)

Merlin? Merlin? *(Looks at the audience.)* How come you can never find a good wizard when you need one? Merlin! *(Turns around really fast as if he were just tapped on the shoulder.)* What was that? *(Tapped on shoulder again.)* Merlin, was that you? Oh, I see, you're invisible again, eh? I told you not to get in a fight with that witch. She's tricky. *(Really excited.)* Look, Merlin, a new princess just moved into the castle next door and I went over to talk to her and she sicked her dragon on me! *(Showing his back.)* Look at these burn marks. I don't know what to do. I'm in love with her. You gotta come up with a magic potion I can use on her. How about the one we used on Rapunzel? Nah, that just made her hair grow. Gosh, I can't believe she turned her dragon on me. Merlin, you should've seen it. It was a mean dragon. Wait a minute. I never heard of a princess that had a dragon. Maybe he's got her held hostage in that castle! Merlin, I know the way to win her heart. Slay the dragon! Now, if you could just tell me where to get a really, really, really, really, really big sword.

Hughston

(Problems with Space Parents)

(Hughston walks up to his parents.)

Mom, Dad, you better sit down. All right . . . uh . . . I ah . . . I got something to tell you and it's bad. Um . . . I'll just say it. Mom, I took out your spaceship without asking and I dented the fender. But it wasn't my fault! There were two robots crossing the galaxy! They just appeared out of nowhere! So to avoid hitting them, I turned right into an asteroid belt. But don't worry. I'm a good driver. I didn't hit a single asteroid. It was the comet I had trouble with. *(Slams fist into hand.)* BAM! I hit it hard. Oh, the spaceship's still in one piece . . . but it looks about as dented as the left side of the moon. Ok, Dad, Mom. I know you have to ground me. But I ask you, please, just don't make me walk to school. That's so 1990's.

Peter

(Look at my Muscles)

Note - This monologue works best for a really skinny kid.
Or a kid that is big for his age.

(Peter is standing on the playground doing an impression of Robert DeNiro.)

Hey you!
You talkin' to me?
Pretty good huh?
I love DeNiro. Eastwood, Stallone, Schwarzenegger.
The Tough Guys.
Like me.
Hey, what are you starin' at?
Ain't you ever seen a handsome dude before?
People have a hard time with me because I'm so perfect.
I mean, how many kids in middle school do you know
who are built like this? Girls love me. It's my big muscles.
Look. *(Flexes his arms.)* Pretty good huh? And I'm only *(Put actor's age in.)*! How did I get this perfect so young? Oh,
you want more? Okay. Prepare yourself. I'm going to
show you my biggest muscle of all. *(Lifts his shirt and shows his stomach.)* One hundred and fifteen pounds of muscle.
Girls love muscles. *(Peter sees a pretty girl.)* Hey girl. You
wanna go out sometime? I'll let you feel my massive
biceps. *(The girl starts to run.)* Hey why are you running?
Some people have a hard time with perfection.

Nathaniel
(No More Baseball, Please!)

(Nathaniel walks up to his dad.)

Dad? I have something I need to tell you . . . No I don't want to go outside and play catch. I want to stay inside and talk. Dad, I've been thinking maybe I shouldn't . . . Look Dad can you put the baseball down? I'm trying to talk. Okay. Where was I? Look I've decided not to play little league this year. Dad? Would you stop laughing. I'm not kidding. No, really I'm not. Dad stop it! I'm quitting baseball. Oh Dad, don't cry. Face it, I'm a terrible baseball player. Last year I struck out thirteen times. And you know I can't catch or pitch. It's true and you know it. The only reason I played for the last couple of years is because I wanted you to be proud of me. But I'm no good in baseball. So I was thinking . . . can you sign me up for soccer?

Paul

(My Best Friend)

Note: In phone monologues, the ". . ." mean that the other person is talking. Try to imagine what they are saying.

(Paul dials the phone.)

(Very cool) Hey Dude what's up?. . . *(Very polite)* Oh, sorry Mrs. Knapp. I thought you were Charlie . . . No you don't sound like Charlie. I guess I just got too much ear wax in my ears or something . . . No, you're right. I'll clean them out as soon as I speak to Charlie . . . So can I speak to him? . . . Thank you, Mrs. Knapp . . . *(Paul waits for Charlie to pick up.)* Dude your mother was strange . . . I don't know, she was all over me 'cause I have too much ear wax. Hey, you want to come over? I got a new skateboard? . . . Oh come on Dude, it will be fun. I'll let you ride my old board . . . No way Dude. I want the new board. It's my board . . . Okay, be that way. I'll just ride both boards by myself . . . Fine, stay home, I don't care. *(Paul hangs up. Then he dials the phone again.)* Hey Mrs. Knapp, can I speak to Charlie again? . . . Thanks . . . Okay Dude, you can ride the new board . . . What do you mean you don't want to? . . . Okay fine, stay at home and play video games. See if I care. *(Paul hangs up again. Then he dials the phone again.)* Sorry Mrs. Knapp, I need Charlie again . . . Dude what video game are you playing? Skateboard 2000? Is that the one where you pretend you're on a skateboard in space? . . . Cool. Can I come over play it with you? . . . Great! Okay Dude, see ya in five."

Austin

(Someone Brought a Gun to School)

(Austin knocks on the Principal's door.)

Mr. Jones, can I talk to you? Look, I've never been to the principal's office before, but I just saw something today I need to tell you about. But you gotta promise you won't tell anybody I told you because the kid I'm gonna tell on is my friend and I don't want anyone to know. He's really a good guy, you gotta remember that. He's just scared 'cause a lot of people pick on him. Promise me you'll remember that Mr. Jones. Okay, here it goes, I just saw, oh this is hard, Jesse Kotch put a gun in his locker. I think he's scared someone's gonna beat him up and he wants protection. But I'm scared someone's gonna get hurt. I've never told on anyone before. But if someone dies, I don't want it to be my fault.

Craig
(My Parents Have Deserted Me)

Note: The quotes, " ", are the letter. The other dialogue is Craig's comments about the letter.

(Craig is sitting on his cot reading a letter he has just received. To audience—)

I've only been at camp two days and already I'm getting a letter from my parents. They probably think I'm home-sick or something. Give me a break. I'm glad to get away from them. I wish I could live at camp and not have to go back to my boring life at home. Well, let's see what my old man and old lady have to say. Hey, maybe they sent me money.

"Dear Craig:

We hope you are having a great time at camp." I am. "You know we worked very hard this year to earn enough money to send you to such a great camp. Every boy should spend one summer of his life riding horses, swimming and living in a cabin. I hope you are grateful." Yeah, whatever. "We worked so hard this year that we are exhausted. So your dad and I decided we TOO need-ed a vacation. So we went to Hawaii!" Go Mom and Dad. "We love it here. The beaches. The sun. The great food.

(cont. next page)

Craig

(My Parents Have Deserted Me cont.)

It's so much better than home. It's peaceful and quiet. Hawaii has been very good for us." I'm so glad my parents are happy. "It's been so good, that we've decided not to leave." What? "That's right we are moving to Hawaii!" Yes! I'm moving to Hawaii! "When I say WE, I mean your father and I. Not you." What? "If you moved here, it would be too much like home. Face it son, you are very loud and messy. In no time at all you would have Hawaii looking as bad as your room back home." I'll be neater. I promise. "Sorry son, it's too late. Well, I've got to go. I have a hula lesson in a couple of minutes. We hope you like camp. Good luck finding a place to live after it is over. We've sold the house. Your stuff is on the front yard in a couple of boxes. Sure hope it doesn't rain. Best Wishes. Your Mom."

Oh no, this is terrible! What am I going to do? *(Craig is getting upset.)* Mom. Dad. I miss them already. *(Craig turns the letter over.)* Wait, what's this. "PS. I was just kidding. We miss you and can't wait for you to come home. Love Mom."

That is so lame. Like they thought I would fall for that. Ha!

Michael

(My Parents are Getting a Divorce)

(Michael is not happy. He's talking to the audience.)

So my day's going just great!
This morning my mom and dad walk into my room
    and say, "Son we need to talk."
So I'm thinking, "Oh no, what did I do?"
Actually I know what I did. I was just hoping they hadn't
    found out about it.
Then my dad says, "Son, your mom and I are getting
    divorced."
Just like that!
He says it like, "Son, your life is over."
Then my mom starts crying.
I hate it when she does that.
Then my dad says, "We want you to know that it's not
    your fault."
And so I start screaming, "Duh, I'm not the one leaving
    my family! I'm not the one deserting my son!"
And that's when my mom really starts crying.
Then my dad says, "Actually son, your mother is
    the one leaving."
It turns out she's an alien from a planet far far away and
    she has to go back to her planet!
Just then my mom rips off her face and she looks just like
    Yoda from Star Wars!
She hugs me goodbye and then walks outside gets in her
    spaceship and flies away! So my day is going just great!

Jeff
(My Brother is Arrested)

(Jeff is talking to the audience.)

My brother, Mark, was arrested yesterday for doing drugs. He and these guys he hangs out with were behind the 7-eleven. This is the third time he's been arrested. My dad says this time he's gonna have to go to jail. My mom cried all last night. My dad was mad and just kept yellin at me. It's not my fault. I don't do drugs. My dad is so upset he can't think straight. He's scared what will happen to Mark when he goes to jail. This is going to totally ruin my brother's life. And all for what? To get high? Drugs aren't worth it.

Richard
(My Muscles Hurt!)

(Richard is talking to the audience.)

Ow, my muscles hurt. I've been lifting these weights my dad got me for Christmas. He says I'm too skinny and I need to put a little meat on my bones. But right now my bones are too tired to stand up. He made me do push-ups, pull-ups, bench presses, and arm curls. I kept yelling "I can't! I can't!" But he said I was being a baby and he made me do them anyway. He says if I don't get muscles, kids at school are going to pick on me and try to beat me up. He says they picked on him a lot when he was little. So he had to get muscles to protect himself. I wish I could go to the store and buy a pair. I kept telling him that kids at school don't want to beat me up. They like me! He says "If you think they like you now, wait till you get muscles. They'll really like you." I think my dad's crazy. I tell him I don't want people to like me for how I look. But for who I am.

Kirk

(Don't Take Me to Mars!)

(Kirk is tied up in a spaceship.)

All right guys, why'd you bring me here? Speak up!
What? . . . You don't speak English? Okay look, I like
your spaceship. It's nice. It's even better than that one
they used in Independence Day. But where are we going?
Tell me! Mars? Pluto? Another galaxy? Just make sure
I'm home in time for school. I've got a big test in science.
We're studying the planets. Hey you! Yeah you with the
three eye-balls. Can you get me a drink of water? I wish
you people would say something. I mean, you're not
people, you're aliens. Hey, what are you guys setting up
over there? What is that? Oh no . . . is that a laser?
Hey! Don't point that thing at me. Oh no! I get it. You
guys are trying to steal all my brain cells. Won't you be
disappointed. I don't have any brain cells. My mom's
always saying my head's full of air. Please don't point that
thing at meeeeeeeee!

Chad

(Math Club is Cool)

(Chad is talking to his best friend, Josh.)

I'm telling you Josh, math club is the best way to get girls
    I've ever thought of.
I'm serious!
Okay, so they ain't models.
But they're GIRLS! . . . Oh yeah, right?
I haven't seen any chicks on your arm lately.
Except maybe your mom.
Let's see how many girlfriends do you have . . . uh . . .
    Zip, Zero, Zilch!

Now my life is zooming.
The math club has turned my life into Baywatch.
Except all the girls are wearing glasses.

Just yesterday I was sitting in math club when Betsy
    walked up and complimented me on my algebra.
Betsy—now that's some fine geometry on a girl.
The square root of Becky is Love. I think she wants me.
$1+1=2$.
Today, I'm going to dazzle her with my word problems.

Okay, Josh, but this Friday night when you're sitting at
    home, alone, remember. Anything times zero is zero.

Travis

(I Want My Best Friend Back)

(Travis is talking to the audience.)

My best friend Guy just got a girlfriend, Tammy. Last week he just walked up to her and asked her out. Just like that. And she said yes. He's very happy. I told him congrats but . . . well, now he spends all his time with her. This weekend he and I were going to the track to race go-carts. But at the last minute he called and bailed on me. He said Tammy wanted him to come over and watch a video. A video? Man, he and I have been saving our money to race go carts for like a year. And bam Tammy calls and . . . all of a sudden he doesn't care about go-carts anymore. And today I asked him if he wanted to come over and hang out. And he said no, he was going to hang out with Tammy. I told him she could come too but he said they wanted to be alone. Alone? He told me I should try to get a girlfriend and then all four of us can hang out. But I don't know. Girls are kind of . . . well I don't know . . . they're girls. This bites! What's the use of having a best friend if you can't spend any time with him?

Glossary of Industry Terms

Show business has its own interesting vocabulary. The word *wings*, for example. When someone tells you to go *stand in the wings*, they mean stand on the *side of the stage*, not on the wings of a bird. I asked a number of the kids I coach to tell me their definitions for some of these important theater/film words. Sometimes kids can explain things more clearly than adults.

AD LIB - To make up words not already in the script. If a director tells you to ad lib, what he means is ignore the script and say something your character would say.

AGENT - A person who helps you get jobs. And then takes 10% of your earnings.

BEAT - A moment. If the script says: A beat, then that means take a small pause before you say your next line.

BLOCKING - Stage Movement. When the director gives you blocking, he is telling you where to stand and when to move.

CENTER STAGE - Right in the middle of the stage.
(see diagram on page 67)

CROSS - When you move from one spot on the stage to another spot. This is like blocking.

CUE - Any signal that it is your turn to speak or move. If the director says "Pick up your cues" he means that when the other actor stops talking you must start more quickly.

Glossary of Industry Terms

CURTAIN CALL - At the end of the play, you come out and bow and wave to your parents.

DIALOGUE - The lines you speak from your script.

DIRECTOR - The person who is in charge of the play or film. He or she instructs the actors, set designers and every other person/part of the play or film.

DOWNSTAGE - The front of the stage closest to the audience. The opposite of Upstage. (see diagram on page 67)

DRESS REHEARSAL - The last rehearsal before the play opens. The actors wear their costumes.

ENTRANCE - To walk on stage.

EXIT - To leave the stage.

FOCUS - Putting all your attention on one thing. If a director yells "focus" they mean "Listen up".

GESTURE - The way you move your arms and hands.

GREEN ROOM - The room where the actors hang out, waiting to go on.

HAND PROPS - Small items used by the actor. A purse or a baseball, for example.

HOUSE - The part of the theater where the audience sits.

IMPROVISATION - Acting without a script. Making it up as you go along.

LINES - The words you speak from the script. Learning your lines means to memorize the speeches your character has in the script.

MONOLOGUE - A character's long speech.

OFF BOOK - Being able to act without your script.

OFFSTAGE - The parts of the stage the audience can't see.

OPENING - The first performance of a play.

PROJECTION - To speak loud enough for the audience to hear you. If the director says *Project*, he means speak louder.

RUN-THROUGH - A nonstop rehearsal of a play.

SIDES - Part of a script. When you audition, they give you sides to read from.

SPOTLIGHT - A bright light.

STAGE LEFT - When you are standing center stage facing the audience, stage left is to your left. (see diagram on page 67)

STAGE RIGHT - When you are standing center stage facing the audience, stage right is to your right. (see diagram on page 67)

TOP - The beginning. When the director says, *Go from the top,* he means start at the beginning.

UPSTAGE - The back of the stage. The opposite of Downstage. (see diagram below)

WINGS - The sides of a stage. If the actor stands in the wings, he is not seen. (see diagram below)

Backstage

Upstage Right	Upstage Center	Upstage Left

W i n g

Center Stage

W i n g

Downstage Center

Downstage Right · · · · · · · Downstage Left

Audience

x x x x x x x x x x
x x x x x x x x x x x
x x x x x x x x x x x x

Bibliography: Magnificent Performances By Young Actors

People often ask me about my favorite performances by young actors. Well, here's my list. No priorities on these. All of them are great study material. Every serious young actor should watch his/her favorites with an eye on the acting techniques displayed.

Henry Thomas in <u>E.T. The Extra -Terrestrial</u> (1982): Watching Henry Thomas trying to hide E.T. is pure comic delight. Watch for a young Drew Barrymore - (PG)

Christina Ricci -<u>The Addams Family</u> (1991) & <u>Addams Family Values (1993)</u>: Her deadpan interpretation of "Wednesday" is both chilling and funny - (Both films PG-13)

Natalie Wood - <u>Miracle on 34th St.</u> (1947): I've seen this film over 50 times. And I never tire of seeing the look in Natalie Wood's eyes when she discovers Kris Kringle is really Santa Claus - (No rating)

Elijah Wood and *Thora Birch* in <u>Paradise</u> (1991): Young love was never so sweet. - (PG-13)

Tatum O'Neal - <u>Paper Moon</u> (1973): It's easy to see why she won an Oscar for this one. Part little girl. Part con-man. She steals every scene she's in. - (PG)

Huckleberry Fox in <u>Terms of Endearment</u> (1983): With just a look he breaks your heart. - (PG)

Macaulay Culkin in <u>Home Alone</u> (1991): There is a reason this is one of the most popular films of all time. And that reason is Macaulay. - (PG)

Travis Tedford in <u>The Little Rascals</u> : The original Little Rascals were big "over" actors. Travis makes Spanky funny and believable.

Sean Nelson in <u>Fresh</u> (1994): Sean Nelson witnesses a playground murder. This film is hard to watch. Very violent. But Sean Nelson's performance is fantastic. - (R)

Ricky Schroder in <u>The Champ</u> (1979): One of the best criers in the business. Boy can this kid shed tears. - (PG)

Hayley Mills in <u>The Parent Trap</u> (1961): The original is still the best. No one plays twins better than Hayley Mills. - (No rating)

Bibliography: Magnificent Performances By Young Actors

Tina Majorino in <u>When A Man Loves A Woman</u> (1994): Tina is an amazing actress.   Definitely one of my favorite performances. - (R)

Zelda Harris in <u>Crooklyn</u> (1994): Zelda plays the only girl in a family with four boys. A strong performance by a wonderful young actress. - (PG-13)

Michael Conner Humphreys in <u>Forrest Gump</u> (1994): Run forest Run. And he does. This kid has what it takes to be a great character actor. - (PG-13)

Anna Paquin in <u>Fly Away Home</u> (1996): She won an Oscar for her work in The Piano. But my favorite performance of hers is in this little known classic. - (PG)

Mary Badham and *Philip Alford* in <u>To Kill a Mockingbird</u> (1962): They are so real it doesn't seem like acting - (No Rating)

Justin Henry - <u>Kramer vs Kramer</u> (1979): He holds his own with Dustin Hoffman and Meryl Streep. - (PG)

Peter Billingsley in <u>A Christmas Story</u> (1983): One of the most rented movies of all time. Peter Billingsley is perfect as the kid who wants a Red Ryder BB gun for Christmas. - (PG)

Peter Ostrum - <u>Willy Wonka and the Chocolate Factory</u> (1971): The best for kids ever made. - Peter Ostrum is the perfect Charlie. - (G)

Jodie Foster - <u>Freaky Friday</u> (1977): Jodie switches personalities with her mother. - (G)

Mara Wilson in <u>Mrs. Doubtfire</u> (1993): All the kids are good in this hilarious film. But Mara Wilson has star power. - (PG-13)

Whittni Wright in <u>I'll Do Anything</u> (1994): She's both adorable and bratty. Not an easy combination to pull off. - (PG-13)

Quinn Cummings in <u>The Goodbye Girl</u> (1977): She's hysterical in this Neil Simon comedy. - (PG)

Patty Duke in <u>The Miracle Worker</u> (1962): She won an Oscar for her amazing portrayal of Helen Keller, a role she also played on Broadway. - (No rating)

The full cast of <u>Bad News Bears</u> (1976): What can you say about these lovable bunch of misfits? Except when I was kid they were my heroes. - (PG)

 Index

Magnificent Monologues for Kids!
&
24-Carat Commercials for Kids!
Everything Kids Need to Know To Break Into Commercials

Postal Orders: Sandcastle Publishing & Distribution, Order Dept., P.O. Box 3070, South Pasadena, CA 91030-6070

Ph./FAX MasterCard/VISA/Am.Express Orders: 800 891-4204
Have your credit card # & expiration date handy.

Internet: WWW.sandcastle-online.com

Trade Distribution: Sandcastle Distribution 323-255-3616
Competitive discount schedule, terms & conditions. Will work from purchase orders then invoice. STOP orders okay. USPS, UPS, Express service available.

Please send the following books . . .

Magnificent Monologues for Kids-$13.95 each   Quantity ____ x $13.95   = _____
24-Carat Commercials for Kids-$14.95 each   Quantity____ x $14.95   = _____

Subtotal = _____

Sales Tax (For CA residents only. Add 8.25% sales tax) = _____
($1.15 per MM4kids book, $1.23 per 24CC4kids book)

Packaging/Shipping: ($3.50 for first book, $0.50/add'l book) = _____

Total = _____

Check included: ☐
Please bill my credit card: ☐ **MasterCard**   ☐ **Visa**   ☐ **Am. Express**

Credit Card #: _ _ _ _ _ _ _ _ _ _ _ _ _ _ _ _

Expiration date: __ __/__ __
Month   Year

_____
Cardholder signature. (We must have your signature to process order.)

Customer Billing Information   *Ship To Information

Name: _____   Name: _____

Address: _____   Address: _____

City: _____   City: _____

State & Zip Code:_____   State & Zip Code: _____

Daytime Phone: ( ) _____

* Please fill in the above if book(s) is to be shipped to someone/somewhere other than customer.